Original title:
The Walnut's Whisper

Copyright © 2025 Creative Arts Management OÜ
All rights reserved.

Author: Olivia Sterling
ISBN HARDBACK: 978-1-80567-321-7
ISBN PAPERBACK: 978-1-80567-620-1

Embraces of Nature's Watchful Eyes

In the garden where squirrels play,
A nutty secret dances all day.
The leaves giggle in the warm, soft breeze,
As laughter echoes through the tall, green trees.

A rabbit hops in a jaunty socks,
Wearing shades and talking to the rocks.
The flowers blush at all the puns,
While bees buzz by like silly, happy buns.

The sun winks down from the sky so blue,
Chuckling softly at the playful crew.
The clouds float by with mischievous grins,
As nature spins tales where the fun begins.

So if you listen to the sounds around,
You'll hear the chuckles hidden in the ground.
Nature's humor is a treasure trove,
Where every creature shares the joy they love.

Echoing Laughter of the Past

In the orchard where shadows play,
Nutty jokes dance in the clay.
The squirrels chuckle with delight,
As branches sway in the twilight.

Old trees groan with tales to share,
Of acorns lost and silly flair.
They tickle the wind with their glee,
Whispering secrets, just like me.

A penguin in a tiny hat,
Danced with rabbits, imagine that!
They rolled and tumbled in the grass,
While farmer's worries came to pass.

The sun sets low; the laughter spreads,
As owls giggle in their beds.
Nature's comedy, a wild jest,
In this orchard, we laugh best.

Beneath a Canopy of Secrets

Beneath branches that twist and twine,
A jester's hat hangs from the vine.
Mice play cards with acorns round,
In laughter's grip, they're happily bound.

The wind whispers jokes no one knows,
As dragonflies flaunt their silly flows.
Grinning foxes share a grin,
While giggling turtles spin to win.

Crickets cheer with their rhythmic hums,
As beetles dance like tiny drums.
Each rustle brings unexpected fun—
Who knew that hay could make them run?

So tuck in tight, enjoy the spree,
For nature's jesters are wild and free.
Beneath this leafy stage we find,
A circus of wisdom, goofy and blind.

Silent Secrets of the Orchard

In the orchard, whispers glide,
Fruitful tales with joy inside.
Beneath the boughs, the giggles rise,
As shadows play with silly sighs.

A raccoon tries its best to juggle,
While a squirrel sends it into struggle.
Nature's whimsy won't forget,
The laughter shared in silly duet.

As owls hoot their best dad jokes,
Even the grumpy hedgehog pokes.
Silly pranks with a twist of fate,
In every laugh, we celebrate!

The trees may whisper and seem discreet,
But their funny tales can't be beat.
Join the chorus, don't delay,
For nature's humor is here to stay!

Beneath the Ancient Canopy

Beneath branches that twist and twirl,
A goat in boots begins to whirl.
Giggling leaves join in the spree,
With secret whispers, wild and free.

The ancient wood hosts tiny plays,
From field mice who deserve the praise.
They act out tales of daring feats,
While underfoot, a party beats.

Peculiar hats on every head,
A parade of laughter being fed.
Jumpy rabbits and snickering bugs,
In this fun theater, they share hugs.

So eavesdrop on the joy around,
Let silly secrets abound.
For under this canopy so grand,
Life's funny moments hand in hand.

Conversations in the Canopy

Up above, the branches dance,
Squirrels chatter, take a chance.
Acorns roll, a nutty race,
Birds sing loud, in their own space.

Frogs leap by with webs on toes,
Twirling leaves, as mischief grows.
The wind just laughs, a playful tease,
Nature's jest, a light-filled breeze.

Echoes of the Woodland Spirit

In the shade, the shadows creep,
Whispers float, a secret heap.
Mice gather round, in a circle tight,
They nibble crumbs from last night's bite.

A fox struts by, with swagger so fine,
Stealing snacks, he drinks the wine.
Bats flit in, making silly sounds,
Echoes bouncing up and down.

Hidden Histories of the Forest

Underneath the ancient trees,
Lies a tale that makes you wheeze.
A tortoise once claimed he could race,
But lost to a snail, at a slow pace!

Mushrooms giggle in a tiny ring,
As the wind comes with a funny fling.
They tell stories of ghosts that roam,
Chasing shadows, but never home.

Secrets Held Tight in Nature's Clutch

A chipmunk grins, with cheeks so wide,
Holding secrets, he just can't hide.
Acorns stuffed, his little stash,
He winks at the trees, in a quick flash.

The brook babbles, with a cheeky glee,
It splashes leaves, as wild as can be.
Nature's humor, in every nook,
A playful mood, the whole day's book.

Chants of the Leafy Dwellers

In the grove where squirrels dance,
A nut parade, oh what a chance!
With acorn hats and cheeky prance,
They laugh and jest, a woodland romance.

The birds join in, they squawk and sing,
About the joy that autumn brings.
A feathery choir, oh how they cling,
To jokes of nuts and other things.

Beneath the branches, shadows play,
As critters gather, bright and gay.
With tales of who stole nuts today,
Their giggles echo, come what may.

When twilight falls, they raise a toast,
A gathering band, they cheer and boast.
Of all the nuts, they like the most,
A chuckling tale, they love to host.

Murmurs of Hidden Connections

Underneath the leafy dome,
A stash of secrets, feel at home.
The giggly breeze makes all things roam,
As whispers tell of nuts named chrome.

The caterpillar sports a grin,
While ants parade in shiny tin.
They joke about the nutty din,
And who will win this nutty win.

In shadows deep, a jest unfolds,
A mystery hidden, yet humor bolds.
Beneath the bark, the story molds,
Of acorns stolen, the laughter holds.

Amidst the chatter, frogs croak loud,
Sharing tales with a merry crowd.
A tie of roots, a laughter shroud,
Connects them all, a giggly cloud.

Soft Echoes of the Resilient Woods

Amidst the trees, a knock you hear,
A woodpecker laughs, never fear.
With every tap, they shed a tear,
Of nutty puns that bring good cheer.

The hedgehogs snicker, round they roll,
As nature's jesters, full of soul.
Wiggling worms share jokes, their goal,
To tickle roots and make them whole.

A rabbit hops with tales in hand,
Of nutty mysteries, oh so grand.
In forest schools, the laughter's planned,
Connections forged in leafy land.

As evening falls, the stars appear,
With whispers sweet, the night is clear.
In every nook, the fun is near,
A woodland rave, let's all adhere!

The Sagas of Verdant Silence

In dappled light, the stories weave,
A nutty epic, so hard to believe.
Squirrels hatch plots, they don't deceive,
In leafy halls, they take their leave.

With secret paths the rabbits hop,
And echoes of laughter, they just can't stop.
Through hidden trails, they skip and bop,
In the trunk's embrace, they truly plop.

The tales of acorns shared at night,
In woodland amphitheaters, pure delight.
The shadows dance, the moon shines bright,
As all who gather, reignite the light.

A chorus rises, delightful and bold,
Of nutty shenanigans, timelessly told.
Within the woods, their spirits unfold,
In laughter's arms, they break the mold.

The Heartwood's Lullaby

In the shade where squirrels tease,
A tree hums soft, like a gentle breeze.
"Hey there, nuts, don't roll away!
I'm just trying to nap, please stay!"

The branches sway with a giggling sound,
While acorns dance upon the ground.
"Who knew naps could be such fun?
Sing along, until the day is done!"

Breaths of the Silent Season

Leaves rustle tales of silly things,
Of jumpy bugs and grasshoppers' wings.
"Should we leap, or just stay still?
Oh, come on, try not to spill!"

Winter whispers through the pine,
"Beware, my snowflakes—do you have a line?"
They flurry and giggle in piles so bright,
"Catch us if you can, oh, what a sight!"

Mysteries Cradled in Humble Corners

In cozy nooks, secrets unfold,
Of acorns' dreams and tales retold.
"Why did the nut cross the log?
To chat with the owl, or just to hog?"

A hedgehog watches, with eyes so wide,
His quills a fortress, he cannot hide.
"His jokes are old, but still a hit,
I'll laugh and roll, I'm here to sit!"

The Quiet Intelligence of Nature

Nature whispers with a cheeky flair,
"Why did the tree grow such wild hair?"
"Maybe it's trying to catch a breeze,
Or hide from the honeyed bees!"

Rabbits giggle, as shadows play,
"Who's the funniest next in ballet?"
With twirls and hops, they take their stance,
"We're nature's clowns, come join our dance!"

Stories Embedded in the Earth

Beneath the soil, tales reside,
Of squirrels who dance and rabbits that hide.
Each nut a secret, a gift from the past,
Giggling roots whisper, their stories amassed.

In shadows they plot, a gathering crew,
With acorn hats and their best leafy shoe.
They hold wild debates, 'Who's the funniest beast?'
As crickets provide the beats for their feast.

The earth laughs softly, a chuckle so deep,
While worms spin yarns that make mushrooms leap.
A playful brigade, the roots intertwine,
In a raucous embrace, they sip sap like wine.

Each step on this patch, a comic retort,
With rascally critters, a lively court.
The tales come alive, through dirt and through grime,
In this merry kingdom, life dances with rhyme.

Mysterious Currents of Rustic Life

In the meadow's embrace, laughter does flow,
Where daisies debate if they should steal the show.
A cow with a grin, wearing shades of delight,
Tries to moo in rhythm, under the moonlight.

The chickens conspire, with their gossiping cluck,
Plotting to prank the old farmer's truck.
While bees do a boogie, in search of sweet blooms,
Buzzing with mischief, their laughter blooms.

Under the oak, where shadows align,
A turtle recites, 'Slow is just fine!'
With a wink and a nod, he goes on his way,
While frogs leap about, in a splashy ballet.

Life teems with quirks, surprises galore,
In rustle and ruckus, there's always a score.
From roots to the sky, all coexist fun,
In this whimsical world, life's never quite done.

The Soliloquy of Age

A wise old tree stands with gnarled embrace,
With bark as a map of time's gentle trace.
He chuckles to leaves, 'Oh, the tales that I know,
Of youthful dandelions, and where the winds blow.'

Squirrels rush past, their antics so spry,
While the tree shakes his head, 'Oh, my! Oh, my!'
'In my younger days, I could juggle the sun,
Now I settle for shade, and watching the fun.'

He whispers to clouds, 'Why dance if you're gray?'
But they twirl and they shift, in a whimsical way.
As critters convene, under branches so wide,
The tree laughs aloud, 'Just take life in stride.'

For with every season, there's joy to be peeled,
In the garden of age, the heart is revealed.
So gather around, let your laughter take flight,
In the glow of the dusk, everything feels right.

Whimsy of the Woven Leaves

A tapestry hangs in the breeze, oh so sly,
With petals and laughter drifting through the sky.
Leaves play dress-up, in colors so bright,
Plotting escapades well into the night.

A breeze comes along, tickles each vine,
Causing a riot, oh how they entwine!
'Let's have a parade!' one bold leaf did call,
And soon every stem joined in to have a ball.

The flowers all giggle, in hues bold and loud,
A conga line forms, a leaf-swaying crowd.
With butterflies joining, all orange and blue,
They twirl and they whirl in nature's grand view.

The forest applauds, with rustles and cheers,
As the leaves jig and hop, casting off fears.
In this carefree realm, with joy we believe,
Every day's a dance, if you dare to perceive.

Frosted Dreams Under the Canopy

Beneath the frost, a secret lies,
A squirrel plotting in disguise.
He dresses nuts in tiny hats,
And giggles with the friendly bats.

The moon is high, the stars are bright,
The critters plan a wild delight.
A dance party by the old oak tree,
With acorns rolling, wild and free.

A misfit crew from near and far,
They crack jokes under the bizarre.
With winter snacks and tales to share,
They frolic with the fresh night air.

So if you hear a raucous cheer,
It's not just fun—it's frosty cheer!
For when the night begins to gleam,
They're living life, not just a dream.

Secrets Entwined in Twilight

In twilight's glow, the laughter flows,
A band of friends with silly prose.
They swap old tales, a drink in hand,
Of stolen nuts and wild plans grand.

A raccoon sings with utmost flair,
While rabbits stomp and dance in air.
The owls hoot in bemused delight,
As shadows spin in giggles bright.

The whispers weave through the dusk,
Of silly tricks and nutty musk.
Each secret shared brings joy anew,
As creatures dream under skies so blue.

So when the twilight starts to creep,
And all is quiet, don't you weep.
For in this hour of soft embrace,
The humor of nature finds its place.

The Language of Leaves

The leaves all chatter in the breeze,
Whispering secrets with such ease.
A rustle here, a giggle there,
They poke fun at the passing air.

The trees are in on this great joke,
With branches swaying, they all poke.
A tumbleweed rolls by to jest,
Claiming he's the very best!

The groundhog grins, he knows the score,
He once wore shoes—couldn't take more!
The petals giggle, pink and bright,
As nature's humor fills the night.

So lean in close and catch the sound,
For nature's chuckle knows no bound.
In every crackle, rustle, and sway,
Lies laughter of leaves in their playful play.

The Silent Sage of Seasons

In the garden dwells a sage so sly,
With knowing gaze and a twinkle in eye.
He watched a worm do a wiggly dance,
And giggled softly at chance romance.

The seasons change, and so does he,
With each new bloom, he tells a spree.
A springtime jest, a winter joke,
With each new whisper, the garden spoke.

He collects the laughter like shining stones,
Each chuckle echoes in grassy tones.
He sways with the wind and nods to the sun,
For every season, there's laughter to be won.

So when you pass his quiet domain,
Listen closely—hear the refrain!
For nature's humor runs deep as roots,
In the silent sage, where joy shoots.

Nature's Journal in Whispered Pages

In the forest, rumors swirl,
Of a heart-shaped treasure, you see,
Squirrels giggle in leafy burls,
Nutty secrets, they're sipping tea.

Rabbits prance in silly shoes,
Chasing shadows, dodging glee,
With each rustle, they could lose,
A nutty game, a jubilee!

Underneath the ancient trees,
Frogs croak out a merry song,
While nature chuckles in the breeze,
This woodland winks, nothing's wrong!

As the sun dips low in grace,
The dance of dusk begins to play,
Each critter in its funny place,
Whispers of joy at the end of day.

Daydreams of the Nutty Protector

A little guard with fluffy fur,
Hides his loot with quite a flair,
Watches over with a little purr,
While giggling at the curious bear.

He wears a hat made of an acorn,
Patrolling paths within the glen,
With woodland friends, he'd never mourn,
Cracking jokes 'til late again!

Chasing tails, they twirl around,
A nutball party, oh what a mess,
Laughter echoes, joy unbound,
Nature's play, a silly fest!

Under stars that wink and sway,
His dreams are full of nuts galore,
In a world where whimsy plays,
A nutty knight forevermore.

Puzzles Held Close in Nature's Heart

Rustling leaves weave riddles bright,
As critters ponder day to night,
A pinecone's face gives quite a fright,
With nutty words that take their flight.

Beneath the branches, secrets sprawl,
Pine needles flutter like a ball,
Each hidden laugh is quite the call,
Nuttiest tales we can install.

Chipmunks whisper, 'What's the trick?'
As squirrels plot to play the slick,
Nature's game, a funny pick,
In cozy corners, mischief thick.

With every glint of sunlit beam,
Solving puzzles is their dream,
In silly costumes, they all gleam,
A merry dance, a joyous theme.

Reveries of the Verdant Sanctuary

In a patch of green, a dance unfolds,
Mice in tuxes, and nuts they hold,
With every twirl, a tale retold,
Of secrets crafted, none too bold.

A mouse named Jake sings silly songs,
While ants march proudly in their throngs,
Laughing as they dodge the wrongs,
Life in the wild where humor belongs.

Frogs hop by with bouncy cheer,
Wearing goggles, they leap quite near,
With nutty schemes, there's nothing to fear,
Nature's laughter, a joy sincere.

As twilight paints the skies in gold,
The sanctuary, with stories told,
In every corner, joy takes hold,
Nutty dreams, in whispers bold.

Wisdom Whispered through Green Leaves

Leaves gossip softly up high,
Tickling branches as they sigh.
Squirrels eavesdrop, tails all aflutter,
While worms roll their eyes, calling it clutter.

Acorns chuckle from their boughs,
Making jokes, 'We're mighty, no how!'
The busy bees buzz with delight,
A raucous party in morning light.

Wind plays tricks with a cheeky dance,
Rustling leaves, giving all a chance.
With laughter echoing through the trees,
Nature's joke box, if you please!

Wisdom sticks, or maybe it flits,
In nature's playground, where humor sits.
Each chuckle shared is bound to thrive,
Turning the forest into a hive!

The Harbor of Woodland Wisdom

In the thickets where shadows blend,
Animals gather, giggles transcend.
Raccoons jest as they count their loot,
While owls wink, not quite so astute.

A fox tells tales of grand escape,
While the rabbits laugh, a funny shape.
Silly deer prance in a silly jig,
Wobbling around—a nature gig!

Log benches are set for a grand old show,
With crickets chirping on the low.
Fungus gives a wink, 'I'm just as wise,'
While mushrooms dance in disguise!

Laughter echoes through the verdant curls,
While wind carries tales of giggling squirrels.
In this harbor of woods, joy anchors tight,
Together, they weave a jolly night!

Shadows Crouching Beneath the Green

Beneath the green, shadows lurk,
Whispering secrets with a smirk.
A hedgehog snickers, sitting in wait,
As hedges shake and mutter fate.

Bunnies plot in conspiratorial glee,
"What if we made a stew from the sea?"
While turtles chuckle, shell's all a-glow,
"Stick to lettuce; that's how we roll!"

A parrot squawks about a lost shoe,
"Who knew greens could be such a zoo?"
With each rustle, a funny tale spins,
Under leaves, where the giggling begins.

Silly shadows dance with intent,
"Let's play hide and seek, we've got time to spend!"
In the cover, they romp and hide,
This woodland world, where laughter glides!

Woven Thoughts of the Earth

On the ground, thoughts weave and spin,
Nature's chatter wrapped in a grin.
Dandelion puffs float on by,
"Let's take a chance, aim for the sky!"

With each seed, a tale takes flight,
Frogs share puns in the pale moonlight.
The soil chuckles, rich and deep,
"Hold on tight! Don't fall asleep!"

A worm hums a tune, joyful and wild,
"Dance with the raindrops, playful and styled."
Every blade of grass joins the tune,
Under the gaze of a cheeky moon.

Thoughts woven like vines intertwined,
Nature's humor perfectly designed.
So come join the laugh, on Earth's merry floor,
Where trees share whispers that you can't ignore!

Twilight Murmurs Amongst the Trees

In dusk's embrace, the leaves conspire,
They giggle softly, as if to inquire.
A squirrel jumps with a comic flair,
Chasing shadows without a care.

A breeze tickles, with playful delight,
Mocking the owls, who blink in the night.
Branches sway, like dancers in glee,
Nature's jesters, wild and free.

Crickets join with their chirpy sound,
While raccoons scuttle, their mischief profound.
In twilight's glow, the antics unfold,
Each rustle a tale, both silly and bold.

Laughter lingers among the trees,
Echoes of whimsy carried on the breeze.
As the stars twinkle, the forest winks,
In this magical world, hilarity links.

Tales Told by the Wind

The wind whispers secrets, so cheeky and bright,
Poking at clouds, creating a sight.
With a whoosh and a swirl, it dances around,
Joking with flowers, beneath it, they bound.

Each gust carries laughter from faraway lands,
Rustling the leaves, like tiny bands.
A kite takes flight, then tips with a spin,
Caught in the humor of the playful wind.

The trees chuckle deeply, their branches entwine,
Sharing wild stories, in rhythm, they rhyme.
With a playful push, they tease and they sway,
As critters below join in on the play.

So listen closely, the breeze does ensue,
With giggles and tales, all fresh and brand new.
For nature's own laughter is never too far,
In the whispers of wind, we find who we are.

The Echo of Autumn's Bounty

Leaves tumble down, with laughter and cheer,
Wearing bright colors, they bring us near.
Acorns drop with a thud, what a sight!
Squirrels dart by, in their playful flight.

Pumpkins grin wide, on porches they sit,
Carved with funny faces, they don't quit.
Cider simmers, the scent fills the air,
An autumnal dance, full of joy and flair.

In this harvest season, the scarecrows smile,
Guarding the fields in a funny style.
As kids leap in piles, of leaves so brown,
Their giggles and shouts echo all around.

So gather the bounty, let laughter resound,
In the autumn's embrace, joy knows no bounds.
With each funny moment, we gather and share,
In this joyous season, love fills the air.

Wisdom Wrapped in Green

In verdant realms, the old trees conspire,
With tales of their youth, that never tire.
Their knots tell a story, of wisdom so deep,
While critters below, in laughter, they leap.

The mossy carpet, a comfy old rest,
Invites weary wanderers, feeling quite blessed.
"A squirrel once stole my last acorn," it groans,
Twisting and swaying, it shares with its bones.

Among branches and leaves, there's humor galore,
As whispers of nature float in through the door.
With laughter and mirth, the forest they fill,
Each turn of the leaf brings a chuckle and thrill.

So heed their wise words, in their silly embrace,
For life is a journey, filled with laughter and grace.
In canopies green, find the lessons they yield,
With fun woven in, let joy be revealed.

Heartbeats of the Forest Floor

In the hush of a tree's tall embrace,
Squirrels debate their next nutty race.
Leaves giggle as they dance in the breeze,
While mushrooms chuckle, whispering tease.

Beneath them, critters plot grand schemes,
A beetle's dream on a bed of leafy dreams.
Frogs leap in rhythm, not quite on time,
To the forest's heartbeat, a laughter-filled rhyme.

Sunbeams tickle the ground in delight,
As shadows play tag with a flash of light.
The ants march proudly, parade in formation,
In the kingdom of crumbs, a sweet celebration.

But oh, what a mess when those acorns fall,
Each thud echoes, a comedic call.
And the wise trees chuckle, how silly it seems,
Nature's own sitcom, or so it deems.

Ancestral Memories in the Dust

Dust dances softly, a twirl of the past,
Whispering secrets, but can't hold them fast.
Grandpa's old boots tell tales of their day,
Of stomps and skips in the glimmering hay.

The old oak tree waves with a chuckle and creak,
Has it seen a snail wearing shoes, oh so chic?
Memories swirl like the leaves that drift down,
As the forest joins in, a whimsical crown.

Crows caw in laughter, they gossip and tease,
About owls who snooze through the loudest of fees.
A squirrel in suspenders shops for some acorns,
While the rabbit keeps losing his theorems of 'bourns'.

In the tapestry woven of bark and of bark,
Each petal a punchline, a spark in the dark.
With the rustling branches, the humor is clear,
Ancestral echoes, forever sincere.

Beneath the Armor of Nature

Beneath thick layers of bark and of leaves,
Lies a goofy gnome with a sack full of thieves.
He dreams of a world where socks find their mates,
Where frogs wear top hats and dance on their plates.

The grasshoppers boast about who's jumpin' the best,
While worms in a band put their rhythm to test.
A ladybug laughs with a wink and a spin,
As butterflies flutter, their dance to begin.

Spiders weave jokes in intricate threads,
About bugs who forget where they've placed their beds.
With a pinch of mischief and a dash of delight,
Nature's grand stage bathes in soft, silly light.

In the armor of forests, fun tales intertwine,
From the silliest critters with hearts so divine.
In every shadow, a giggle awaits,
A world full of laughter at Nature's own gates.

The Murmur of Forgotten Seasons

Seasons whisper quietly, jokes from the past,
A snowflake's waltz, maybe not meant to last.
The autumn leaves laugh as they twirl and fall,
While winter's too busy with snowball brawls.

Now spring brings a chuckle with every new bloom,
As flowers plan parties, oh boy, what a room!
The summer bugs buzz with a comedic flair,
As they bicker for space in the sun's golden air.

A song of each season, a playlist, you see,
From winter's cold blues to summer's spree.
The trees double over, their laughter unfolds,
Chasing the leaves that the playful wind holds.

Forgotten seasons, they giggle and play,
Reminding us all, life's a comical sway.
With each tick of time, they dance on repeat,
Nature's own humor, a rhythm so sweet.

Conversations of Quiet Kinship

In the shade they sit and grin,
Gossiping where tales begin.
Nutty puns and jokes take flight,
Bouncing laughter, pure delight.

Branches sway in rhythmic cheer,
Oldest secrets, crystal clear.
Oh, how they chuckle, it's a show,
Telling tales of long ago.

The sun dips low, their shadows play,
Oh what mischief! Come what may!
With every rustle, cheeky glee,
Echoes of their harmony.

As daylight fades, they stretch and yawn,
Skeletal limbs adorned with dawn.
A whispered joke, they intertwine,
Surely, laughter's the best sign.

Hidden Harmonies Underneath the Sky

Beneath the stars, they softly chime,
Their rustling leaves keep perfect time.
Jokes a-plenty, a riotous election,
Combining wisdom with misdirection.

Swinging branches share a tale,
Of acorns lost and a daring gale.
What a sight, these jolly souls,
Conspiring to play the day's roles.

Clouds above, they cheer and scoff,
Ticklish winds that never doff.
A melody of whirls and twirls,
Nutty laughter rings and swirls.

And under moonlight, dreams take flight,
With goofy shadows, what a sight!
Joined in guffaws till the break of day,
Revelry in their silly ballet.

Ponderings of the Oldest Oak

Oh, ancient one with wisdom vast,
In your branches, memories cast.
You contemplate, with a wink or two,
The folly of leaves as they bid adieu.

"Remember when, just last fall's breeze,
You lost a few to the mischievous tease?"
A swirling dance, the gusts they know,
Sending you spinning, a light-hearted show.

The squirrels giggle in the chatter,
For every acorn that's bound to splatter.
Each pondered whisper, a giggle entwined,
Creating echoes that spark the mind.

So raise your voice, though it be soft,
Mock the fables that drift aloft.
In your laughter, life takes root,
Direction found in each nut's pursuit.

The Sighing of Time-Worn Trees

Listen close; can you hear their sighs?
A secret world where humor flies.
Their gnarled limbs knot in wise debate,
Old tales sprinkled with love and fate.

They chuckle at the passing breeze,
Imagine what life could be with ease.
Twisted roots in playful pranks,
A game of giggles, mischievous thanks.

Fallen leaves in a carefree show,
Painting the ground with a humorous flow.
The dance of nature, frolic and play,
In laughter's embrace, they find their way.

And as the sun dips low and dims,
They share a toast with the twilight whims.
A forest chuckle as night descends,
Time-worn trees, the best of friends.

Unveiling the Forest's Enigmas

In the woods where secrets sprout,
Trees wear hats and dance about.
Squirrels gossip, acorns fly,
Mice wear boots and never lie.

Birds recite their poems loud,
In feathers bright, they form a crowd.
Roots tickle toes as you pass by,
Nature's joke—oh, my oh my!

With every rustle, laughter sneaks,
Woodland critters play hide-and-seek.
A tree stump grins, and leaves all cheer,
The forest sings—a raucous sphere.

In this realm of chuckles grand,
Every twig and branch has planned.
So come and join the merry spree,
Nature's jest is wild and free!

The Language of Twilight's Embrace

As twilight drapes the world in hues,
Bats exchange their cartoonish views.
Owls wear glasses, whizzing by,
Counting stars with a twinkling eye.

Fireflies wink in a cosmic dance,
"Is that a bug or just a chance?"
A hedgehog sighs, "I don't complain,
Just rolling around in my own lane!"

Crickets chirp a silly tune,
While shadows play beneath the moon.
Mysteries wrapped in giggles bright,
Nature's secrets shared at night.

Embrace the laughs in twilight's fold,
Every shadow has stories untold.
Join the fun this night so sweet,
Where every turn brings laughter's beat!

Whispers of Ancestors in the Canopy

Up in the trees, a tale unfolds,
Old spirits giggle, secrets told.
Ghosts of acorns, laughter in the breeze,
Tickling leaves and shimmying trees.

"Once we were giants!" a branch does claim,
"Now we're all just part of the game!"
Their chuckles flutter through the air,
While squirrels debate without a care.

Barking at stars, the branches prance,
With every rustle, they take a chance.
Ancestors' wisdom wrapped in glee,
Trees are wise but love to be free.

So listen close, and you might find,
Ancient jokes that twinkle and rewind.
In the canopy, a party's alive,
Where age meets mirth and squirrels thrive!

Enigmas Beneath the Gnarled Roots

Beneath the roots, where mischief brews,
Worms host meetings with pointy shoes.
Gnarled limbs whisper in earnest tones,
Raccoons with sass play on their phones.

"Have you heard the one about the leaf?"
The mossy floor erupts in disbelief.
As snails unfold their scrolls of wit,
Each inch of laughter—nothing's a hit!

Underfoot, a party rages on,
Ants don tuxes until the dawn.
Every pebble has a pun to share,
Rooted joy sprawls everywhere.

So come and dig where riddles lie,
In tangled roots, let out a sigh.
Nature's humor, quirky and stout,
In the soil, joy sprouts out!

Echoes of Ancient Timber

In the forest, a nut took flight,
Rolling downhill with all its might.
It giggled and chuckled with every bump,
While the trees swayed, their branches thump.

A squirrel chased fast, but tripped on a stone,
Landing headfirst on a throne of his own!
The acorn giggled, what a silly sight,
As the trees laughed on in the afternoon light.

The wise old oak shared a secret to share,
'Just roll with it, don't you dare despair!'
So the walnut danced, twirled, and spun,
A show for the critters, oh wasn't it fun!

With whispers of folly, the woods came alive,
Laughter echoed, causing joy to thrive.
Even the wind poked fun with a breeze,
In this whimsical dance among ancient trees.

Secrets in the Shell

Beneath the shell, a secret lies,
A nutty joke with twinkling eyes.
It said, 'I'm cracking up, oh what a tease,'
While leaves just shivered, grinding their knees.

Two turtles debated the weight of the nut,
While squirrels just gathered, 'What's this all about?'
They tossed it around like a hot potato,
Over peas and carrots, a nutty tornado!

A wise old bat flew by with a grin,
'What's in there, friends? A riddle or sin?'
But the nut just chuckled, feeling so sly,
'Come closer, dear bat, I can't tell you why!'

Each creature around shared their wittiest jest,
While the walnut just sat there, enjoying the fest.
It whispered sweet nothings, but all in good fun,
As the secrets within remained hidden, just one.

The Silent Grove's Confession

In a grove where silence dared to creep,
A nut confessed, 'I can't take this sleep!'
It wobbled and giggled, spun round for a laugh,
While branches would sway, oh, what a gaffe!

A rabbit chimed in, 'Come on, little friend,
Life's too short for nonsense to end!'
But the nut just wobbled, saying with glee,
'I prefer to roll, it's easier for me!'

Underneath a moonbeam, creatures all peered,
Wondering what secrets their walnut had steered.
With a wink and a twist, it danced in its shell,
'You'll never guess my nutty tales—I wish you well!'

As the crusty bark creaked, the owls lined the row,
Giggles erupted from the roots down below.
In the silent grove, humor took its place,
Amidst whispers and chuckles, there was a nut's grace!

Beneath the Canopy of Dreams

Beneath the leaves where dreams take flight,
A walnut sighed, 'Oh, what a night!'
It rolled on the grass, what joy to explore,
While stars twinkled tales of yore.

A chipmunk strolled, curious and spry,
Said, 'Have you ever learned how to fly?'
The walnut just winked, with confidence beamed,
'Just trust in the breeze, or so it seems!'

The earthworms were laughing, the crickets held sway,
As the moon started rapping in its own funny way.
'Let's party,' they cried, 'the night's just begun!'
While the walnut nodded, delighting in fun.

Under skies shimmering with dreams all around,
The forest was filled with the softest of sound.
And the walnut, with mirth, shared its silly schemes,
Leaving long echoes beneath starry beams.

Revelations from the Rooted Realm

In the garden, nuts do plot,
Sneaking snacks, they think they're hot.
With cheeky smiles, they crack a joke,
While squirrels dance and acorns smoke.

The trees all giggle, swaying free,
Revealing tales of nutty glee.
Raspberry bush grins down low,
While daisies nod, "Let's steal the show!"

From twigs and leaves, laughter flies,
In every shadow, mischief lies.
A hidden dance, all wild and bright,
As fireflies join in the moonlight.

A root's own secret, pure delight,
Those tiny pranks bring pure sunlight.
For in this place, alive with cheer,
Every nut has a story here.

The Subtle Symphony of the Orchard

Beneath the boughs, on a merry day,
Acorns tap-dance, come what may.
With a wink and a nutty grin,
They stage a show, let the fun begin!

From branches high, the laughter rings,
As little bugs play out their flings.
A playful breeze, the sun's delight,
Frolicsome sounds from morning to night.

A blossom giggles, sways with flair,
While birds debate, 'Who's got the best hair?'
Nuts scatter secrets in hushed tones,
In the cool shade, no need for bones.

Each fruit in this orchard sings a tune,
As flowers burst out, making room.
With every tickle of grassy space,
Joy blooms wide, wild as the chase.

Murmurs from the Mystic Wood

In twilight's glow, the leaves all converse,
Nutty creatures rehearsing their verse.
They wink at moonbeams, plot their scheme,
A dodgy dance is their sweet dream.

Roots tap gently beneath the ground,
While mushrooms chuckle, spinning around.
Squirrels gossip—who's lost their stash?
While a sleepy owl lets out a crash!

From old bark, stories come alive,
Tales of naughtiness, how they thrive.
The wind can't help but chuckle along,
In this hidden haven, nothing feels wrong.

Echo of giggles blend with the leaves,
As mystery swirls and mischief weaves.
The creatures of dusk, around they twirl,
In a funhouse of nature, let laughter unfurl.

Chronicles of the Forgotten Grove

In the nooks where shadows play,
Whispers bounce and twist away.
A nut so bold, he takes the lead,
Telling tales of mischief and speed.

The mossy floor dances in delight,
While dragonflies dart, oh, what a sight!
With a chuckle here and a snicker there,
Nature rejoices, full of flair.

Old branches creak, a merry tune,
As fireflies gather beneath the moon.
Each cranny holds a story crazy,
In this wacky grove, conditions are hazy.

So come along, let your heart take flight,
In a land of giggles, feels just right.
For every nut knows, as night's unfurled,
This secret laughter lights up the world.

The Cacophony of Calm

In a garden full of chatter,
Squirrels argue, who's the fatter.
Birds sing tunes with squirrelly flair,
Yet a silence hangs in the air.

A gopher's laugh, a rabbit's dance,
Nature seems to take its chance.
A breeze slips by, it shouldn't dare,
But the trees are tickled—what a scare!

Leaves giggle at the silly strife,
As critters play at living life.
From acorns small to mighty oaks,
All share secrets, all share jokes.

So when calm reigns with such delight,
Do you dare to join the fight?
Or sit back, chuckling, no alarm,
In this cacophony so warm.

Whispers in the Wind's Embrace

The wind spills secrets, oh so sly,
As dandelions wave goodbye.
A gust of laughter in the air,
With every step, a tickle, where?

Trees shake hands with cups of dew,
While curling leaves play peekaboo.
The sun sneezes on a passing snail,
And bumbles buzz with tales to tell.

With each soft brush of playful breeze,
The grass joins in, 'Oh, please, oh, please!'
A chorus builds, both loud and light,
As nature chuckles, pure delight.

So dance along on paths so wide,
Embrace the world, it's fun to bide.
With whispered giggles all around,
In this embrace, our joy is found.

Voices from the Forest Floor

Down below where mushrooms grow,
The ants discuss who's faster, though.
A beetle boasts and puffs his chest,
While crickets chirp, they know the best.

The soil chuckles, rich and deep,
A true gem, no time for sleep.
With each small step of tiny feet,
A hilarious tune, a rhythmic beat.

In this noisy realm of roots and sprout,
Fun is the aim, there's little doubt.
A snail like an artist, slow to glide,
Crafts the best graffiti, full of pride.

So gather round in shadiest spots,
Where laughter jives and fun never rots.
Voices rise from the forest floor,
In this merry crew, who could ask for more?

Messages Encased in Wood

Once there lived a tree so wise,
With bark that held a great surprise.
It carved out tales of every day,
A little bird's laughter in dismay.

"Why do you laugh?" asked a passing bee,
"Your stories are all about me, me, me!"
The tree just giggled, roots winking bright,
"Every tale's worth a silly flight!"

The breeze carried the wisdom near,
"I'm just a tree, without a beer!"
Oh what a ruckus, how they roared,
When woodland creatures huddled and stored.

So if you wander past that old tree,
Remember, it laughs, it's always free.
With messages encased in wood,
As funny as it ever could.

Tales of the Hidden Grove

In the grove where shadows play,
The squirrels dance without delay.
They chatter loud, and then they stop,
To watch a leaf take quite a flop.

A raccoon with a shiny tin,
Claims he'll win, but can't begin.
He swipes the snacks and takes a bow,
All while a bird just says, "Oh wow!"

With every gust, the branches creak,
And branches swing like a hide-and-seek.
A chipmunk sneezes, then runs away,
Leaving all the trees to have their say.

Oh, what fun this grove can be,
With giggles floating from each tree.
In this playful, leafy place,
Nature's laughter fills the space.

Echoes of the Timeless Tree

Underneath that ancient oak,
A wise old bird begins to croak.
He tells tall tales of days gone by,
While butterflies just flutter by.

The branches wiggle, leaves shake free,
The wise old owl hoots, "What's the key?"
But all the whispers get mixed up,
As squirrels sip from a happy cup.

A rootsy debate breaks out in tune,
While frogs croak loud beneath the moon.
"Who's the oldest?" one tree shouts,
While insects buzz and jump about.

Echoes rise and fall, what glee,
Nature's chatter fills the spree.
Even the ants can't keep the score,
They march in circles, wanting more!

Secrets in the Shell

A little critter hugs his shell,
He giggles soft; oh, what a spell!
When it rains, he plays a game,
Splashing water, never the same.

The tortoise teases from afar,
"Bet you can't reach that shiny star!"
But the snail just grins and takes his time,
Saying, "Slow and steady—feels just fine!"

With little paws tapped on the ground,
A secret dance began to sound.
The shell spins round, what a delight,
Bringing smiles under moonlight bright.

And when the sun begins to rise,
The critters open sleepy eyes.
They know that laughter fills the air,
In the garden, without a care.

The Soft Voice of Nature

In the morning mist, a whisper plays,
The wind hums sweet in gentle ways.
All the trees join in a song,
While the rabbits bounce along.

Caterpillars wiggle, can't sit still,
A game of tag is such a thrill.
"Catch me if you can," they say,
As butterflies flit and sway.

The breeze declares a funny tale,
About a snail that missed a trail.
"Slow down there," sings a bright small thrush,
"Life's a race, but don't rush!"

So in this meadow, hearts align,
With laughter ringing, oh, divine!
Each creature shares a joyful tune,
Nature's music, morning's boon.

Tales of the Nut-bearing Guardians

In the orchard where squirrels play,
Nuts chatter secrets, bright as day.
A squirrel pops in, with a nutty grin,
Claiming his kingdom, let the fun begin!

A rabbit hops by, with a quirk in his ear,
Rolling his eyes, he joins in the cheer.
"What's the big deal?" says a wise old crow,
"It's just a nut party, don't be so slow!"

With each crinkle and crack, laughter ignites,
As the guardians dance through the warm summer nights.

A dance-off ensues, with nuts in the air,
Who knew these critters could cause such a flare?

So next time you see, a nut on the ground,
Know it's a secret, full of joy all around.
The guardians giggle, both sly and spry,
In nutty adventures, they always fly high!

Voices of the Verdant Veins

In the shade of the leaves, the whispers do flow,
Like gossiping trees in an emerald show.
"Have you heard the one?" asks a vine with a twist,
"About the nut bandit? Oh, dear, do not miss!"

The flowers all giggle, their petals aglow,
As the grass joins in with a soft, silly blow.
"Remember the time a nut rolled too fast?
It danced on the breeze, what a riotous blast!"

The roots laugh below, holding stories galore,
Of nutty escapades, and so much more.
"Let's gather the tales, for the next soirée,
With nut muffins and jokes, let the fun sway!"

As twilight sets in, stars begin to twinkle,
The voices grow louder, all the critters sprinkle.
Together they sing, in a nutty refrain,
A chorus of laughter, like sweet summer rain!

Reinventions in the Rain's Caress

Pitter patter here, the nuts start to leap,
Making new shapes in a puddle so deep.
"Oh look, it's a boat!" shouts a bold little sprout,
"Quick, grab your paddles, we're sailing out!"

A chipmunk dives in with a splash and a laugh,
Guiding this vessel with a zest for the craft.
"Watch out for the waves, they splatter and spray!
This sea of adventure will carry the day!"

As raindrops fall down, they turn into jests,
A twirl of the nut leaves, a sweet little fest.
The world's a circus, a comical stage,
With each little storm, they turn a new page!

So if you find nuts, in the rain's merry dance,
Join in the fun, give adventure a chance.
For when it rains laughter, you'll see it is clear,
Life's nutty escapades are always so dear!

Magic Encased in Time's Shell

In a shell of surprise, a magic unfolds,
A nut with a secret, a story untold.
"Crack me open, folks, and you'll see what I got,
A treasure of humor, in a playful plot!"

The crowd gathers 'round, with their eyes open wide,
As the nut gives a wink, full of spirit and pride.
"I'm not just a snack, oh no, not today,
I've got somersaults and puns on display!"

With a flip and a twirl, the nut starts to shine,
Transforming the field into a grand nutty line.
"Let's dance and frolic, make merriment swell,
For magic is simply a fun little shell!"

So if you encounter this nut on your way,
Remember the giggles and join in the play.
For life is a circus, with laughter to tell,
And magic lies hidden in each lovely shell!

The Echoing Heartbeat of the Earth

In the yard where laughter flows,
A little seed wore tiny clothes.
With each soft bump and gentle thud,
It danced around, a silly bud.

Its roots would jiggle with delight,
As ants performed a wobbly flight.
Oh, gravity, a friend so bold,
Keeps stories hidden and retold.

The world would shake, the plants all grin,
As worms would twirl beneath their skin.
Each rustling leaf began to sing,
A chorus loud, from early spring.

So let us laugh, while grass does sway,
In rhythms strange that lead the way.
For nature's heart beats wild and free,
A funny tune, just wait and see!

Tales of Green Guardians

Once a tree wore glasses thick,
Advising leaves with every trick.
"Don't lean too close, be wise my dear!"
Yet branches still had much to cheer.

The critters gathered for a show,
A squirrel danced, putting on a glow.
He twirled and leaped near roots so wide,
His friends all laughed; he was a guide.

The flowers swayed, with colors bright,
Cheering on with pure delight.
The tree just sighed, a wise old sage,
While all around, the fun turned page.

In leafy whispers, secrets spun,
Of silly pranks and playful fun.
So join the dance, don't miss the beat,
Where guardians laugh, and life's a treat!

Memoirs of a Nut-Laden Autumn

One nut declared, "I'm quite the snack!
I'll roll and bounce; no need to pack!"
But down the hill, it took a dive,
In search of friends; oh, how they thrived!

Acorns gathered with a cheer,
Telling tales of joyful fear.
"Our friends are wise, they hide so well,
But I once tripped—oh, what a spell!"

The wind would blow, their stories spun,
As giggles echoed just for fun.
With every crunch, a hearty laugh,
In nut-sized dreams, they found their path.

So autumn speaks in hushed delight,
While critters play till fall turns night.
With memories sweet, they roll away,
In nutty joy, throughout the day!

The Gentle Song of the Old Tree

An old tree hummed a tale so grand,
Of breezy days and sandy strands.
"Once I was young, a sprout on spree,
But now I sway, just listen to me!"

The squirrels paused to hear him sing,
With fluffy tails, they danced in spring.
"Life's full of twists, just take some notes,
In laughter, even whispers floats!"

The branches waved like seasoned pros,
With rustling leaves that tickled toes.
"Don't fret too much, let worries flee!
For every shadow, there's a tree!"

In every creak, a giggle leapt,
As nature's rhythm softly crept.
So join the song, let laughter ring,
In every bark, the joy they bring!

The Narrative of Nature's Adornments

In a forest dress, the trees do prance,
Leaves in a tango, taking their chance.
Squirrels hold parties, in golden light,
Guarding their treasures, what a sight!

Mushrooms wear hats, quite out of style,
While crickets chirp, with a wink and a smile.
Rabbits in bow ties, hop with great flair,
Nature's a circus, beyond compare!

Flowers gossip, 'Did you see that bee?'
Spreading their rumors, hoping to be free.
Clouds roll in laughing, with a thunderous clap,
It's a wild banquet, with no time for a nap!

So gather your joy, beneath the tree's shade,
Where giggles and whispers surely won't fade.
In this wacky world, where laughter's the prize,
Nature's adornments wear comical guise!

Whispers of Shaded Shadows

Under the branches, a chatter so sly,
Critters conspiring, as clouds drift by.
"Did you hear the news?" one squirrel did squeak,
"Berries are ripe—grab a snack, take a peek!"

The shadows dance lightly, in playful delight,
While ants form a queue, to celebrate night.
Owls hoot in jest, perched high up above,
Sharing their wisdom, with giggles of love.

The breeze tells a tale, of branches that sway,
As trees bend their limbs, in a silly ballet.
Each rustle a whisper, a jest that they share,
In the depths of the forest, it's laughter and care!

So come hear the stories, the secrets profound,
Whispers of shadows, in silliness drown.
Let nature's humor warm your hearts anew,
In the theater of smiles, created just for you!

Harmonies of the Harvest Moon

Under the harvest moon, the owls are grand,
Playing their flutes with a feathered hand.
Pumpkins wear hats, looking quite goofy,
While ghosts at the party get all loopy!

Bats do a jig, on a crisp autumn breeze,
And scarecrows dance, with a shivering ease.
The nightingale hums, a tune oh so sweet,
As crickets keep rhythm, tapping their feet.

Cider in barrels, bubbling with glee,
Join in the fun, come dance with me!
The moon's shining brightly, casting a spell,
On the merry menagerie, a charm we can tell!

So round up your critters, let's shout out a cheer,
For the harvest moon's laughter, we hold dear.
With harmonies ringing, let's toast to the night,
In this folly of joy, everything feels right!

The Enigma of the Leafy Veins

Leaves like mosaics, colors divine,
Whispering secrets in a twisty line.
"Why did the branch break?" a wisecrack would say,
"Too much leaf gossip, it just couldn't stay!"

The beetles are bouncers, keepers of style,
Regulating parties with a glimmer and smile.
"Here's the guest list," a ladybug shouts,
As caterpillars wiggle and strut about.

Sunlight's a DJ, spinning good vibes,
While ants serve refreshments, oh how time flies!
Frogs croak their laughter, a ribbiting cheer,
In leafy enigma, joy's always near.

So come bear witness, a spectacle bright,
In nature's green ballroom, where all is delight.
With every soft rustle, the jesters will sway,
In the enigma of veins, we'll dance the night away!

The Dance of Leaf and Light

In the orchard, leaves giggle bright,
Dancing under the sun's warm light.
They twirl and sway, oh such delight,
While shadows play, a funny sight.

A squirrel trips, lands on a branch,
Wobbling, wobbling, what a chance!
He takes a bow, missteps enhance,
Nature's stage, an unlikely dance.

The breeze joins in, a merry band,
Whistling tunes, it takes a stand.
Causing chaos, oh so grand,
Leaves chuckle softly, oh, so planned!

The sun dips low, a curtain call,
With giggles echoing through it all.
Nature's show, we've had a ball,
In the orchard, laughter stands tall.

Timeworn Secrets of the Orchard

Old branches creak, they're telling tales,
Of fruity escapades and tiny trails.
The winds carry giggles, like playful gales,
Secrets that make you laugh without fails.

Beneath the boughs, a raccoon sneaks,
With a patchy coat and muddy cheeks.
He grabs a nut, oh what a freak,
Fumbles and tumbles, oh, how he peaks!

The apples blushed, they knew the score,
As squirrels plotted, their nutty war.
They twitched their tails, their spirits soar,
While shadows stretched, wanting more.

Whispers of laughter in dusk's soft glow,
Carry along merriness, and flow.
Timeworn secrets that endlessly show,
Nature's humor, a playful show!

Voices Carved in Nature's Embrace

Bark etched with laughter, stories abound,
Every groove holds a joy unbound.
Trees gossip softly, a whimsical sound,
In nature's embrace, hilarity found.

A crow cracks jokes, perched up high,
While acorns giggle as they fall shy.
They bounce around, oh me, oh my,
Who knew a forest could make you cry?

With wind-chime whispers, oh so sly,
They plot their pranks as time drifts by.
Nature's laughter, it won't die,
Echoes of joy beneath the sky.

As shadows dance, persisting play,
Among the trees where children sway.
Voices carved, their own ballet,
In nature's arms, forever stay!

The Language of Gnarled Branches

Gnarled branches twist, they start to speak,
In a dialect of chuckles, unique.
They bend and bow, oh so cheek,
Creating laughs with every tweak.

The owl hoots softly, joining in fun,
With wisdom brewed under the sun.
He rolls his eyes, a witty pun,
As laughter ripples, a charming run.

These quirky limbs, nature's own crew,
Enact their tales, strange yet true.
With snickers hidden, a playful view,
A language shared, we feel anew.

As twilight descends, the giggles blend,
With stars that wink, on laughter they depend.
In the timbered grove, there's no end,
To the language of joy, we comprehend!

Rustling Tales of Roots

In a garden green, they dance and sway,
Little roots giggle in their own way.
Tickled by rain, they jive in bliss,
As worms play tag, how could they miss?

The sun peeks in with a mischievous grin,
"Hey, little sprouts, let's begin!"
With leaves all fluttering, they shout with glee,
"We're not just plants; we're a family tree!"

Pigs in the mud, they can't sit still,
"Care for a dance? Just use your will!"
The carrots laugh out from below the ground,
"Is this a party? Well, look at us bound!"

So gather 'round, in this leafy grove,
Where every little thing likes to rove.
In the rustling tales of laughter's flight,
Every root whispers fun, day and night.

A Story Etched in Bark

In the forest tall, where the silly squirrels play,
A tree tells a joke, in its own witty way.
"Why did the bird sing and dance on a wire?"
"Because what else would it do? It's not one to tire!"

With bark like a notebook, it notes every jest,
Leaves flutter giggles, they're laughing the best.
Yet pinecone gigglers chime in for the show,
"Don't forget the acorns! They'll steal the show!"

Oh, the ants march in, with their tiny parade,
Carrying crumbs of snacks that they've made.
The tree just shakes, in laughter profound,
"Hurry up, little ones, or you'll miss the sound!"

And as night falls in, the stars wink anew,
A tale etched in bark, for the forest crew.
With laughter and joy, the night takes flight,
In this woodland tale, we dance till the light.

Shadows of the Woodland Heart

In the shadows deep, where the woods like to laugh,
You'll find mischievous sprites on their playful path.
Bouncing with joy, on mushroom tops,
Tickled by breezes, they twirl and hop.

A wise old owl, perched up so high,
Hoots out the secrets of how to fly.
"Just flap your wings, don't take it to heart!"
The sprites giggle loud, playing their part.

The bushes shake when a rabbit appears,
With oversized ears, it lends out its cheers.
"Join in the fun, don't stand there so shy!"
And all woodland creatures just laugh till they cry.

As shadows dance softly, under the moon,
Laughter rings out like a merry tune.
In this heart of the woods, where joy takes its flight,
The shadows are filled with pure delight.

Whispers From the Hollow

In the hollow deep, where the secrets reside,
Laughter and mischief go hand in hand wide.
Crickets chirp tales, as frogs jump about,
And the whole forest joins in with a shout.

"Why did the hedgehog cross over the hill?"
"Who knows! For a laugh, or maybe a thrill?"
Beneath twisted roots, the bunnies all grin,
Pondering on, what tricks they'll begin.

With a fluttering page of leaves turning round,
The wind carries tales from the ground to the mound.
"Hey, little friends, come gather real close,
Let's share our jokes, a storytelling dose!"

From gnarled old branches, the whispers cascade,
Tickling the ears of the friends that parade.
In this hollow of laughter, where fun takes a seat,
Every whisper resounds, "Life is a treat!"

The Hum of the Ancient Earth

In a forest of secrets, under leaves so green,
An old tree chuckles, oh what a scene!
Its roots have stories, they giggle and sway,
While critters conspire, to dance and to play.

A worm in a wig, he's quite the shady chap,
With his wormy pals, they plot and they map.
A crow with a beak full of wisecracks so loud,
Makes the leaves tremble, he's drawing a crowd.

The sun winks down with a glittery grin,
While squirrels debate, should they let the fun begin?
A jester of nature, the breeze starts to tease,
And laughter erupts from the branches and leaves.

So come join the ruckus, let worries disperse,
In the realm of the ancient where chuckles rehearse.
For nature's a stage with a cast so absurd,
Each rustle and giggle, a whimsical word.

Fables Twisted in Twigs

Once a twig claimed it held the best tales,
Of bold little critters who rode on the gales.
But the ants, they just laughed, 'twas all in good fun,
For everyone knew, the twig weighed a ton!

A spider spun stories with shimmering silk,
Of brave little beetles who came out at milk.
But a grasshopper piped in, with a hop and a bounce,
'Your fables are sticky, as thick as a pounce!'

Then a snail with a shell, quite grand in design,
Said, "Time is a treasure, and I'm taking mine!"
While the fireflies flickered their giggly delight,
They turned the night dark into a festival bright.

Amidst all the chatter, the woods sang their song,
Where legends are woven, both silly and strong.
So gather 'round closely, let imaginations swing,
For the twigs have their fables, and laughter's the king.

Echoes of Earthy Reverie

In a glade full of whispers, a butterfly spun,
Chasing sweet secrets beneath the warm sun.
A rogue little gopher hopped high in the air,
Said "Catch me if you can," with a mischievous flair.

The mushrooms stood tall, in their polka-dot caps,
Chiding one another with quips and mishaps.
A fox rolled his eyes, he was clearly bemused,
As the critters engaged in their nutty ruse.

The daisies had gossip of bees and their schemes,
While the willows crooned soft, in their swaying dreams.
"Oh, what a jest!" laughed the wind with a swirl,
"Worlds collide rhythmically, just let it unfurl!"

So dance in the shadows, embrace all the cheer,
For nature's a jester, with tales to endear.
In the echoes of laughter, let your spirit soar,
As the earthy reverie calls for encore!

Threads of Time in Nature's Tapestry

Once a dandelion puffs, with a chuckle and grin,
Said, "Look at my friends, we are floaters of wind!"
But the thistle just snorted, "You think you're so grand,
With your fluff and your fluffies, go back to your sand!"

The oak tree chuckled, its bark full of knots,
As squirrels scurries, debating their spots.
"Who lives in the past?" an owl hooted proud,
While the moon winked down, nestled soft in a cloud.

A caterpillar complained of the weight of his years,
"Change is so heavy, it fills me with fears!"
But's suddenly gleaming, with colors so bright,
Each thread weaves a tale throughout day and night.

With stitches of laughter, and patches of fun,
Nature's a quilt, stitch it endlessly, run!
Through the fabric of time, let joy intertwine,
In this tapestry woven, laughter's divine!

www.ingramcontent.com/pod-product-compliance
Lightning Source LLC
Chambersburg PA
CBHW071853160426
43209CB00003B/529